There's No Place
Like the Internet
in Springtime

There's No Place Like the Internet in Springtime

Erik Kennedy

Victoria University Press

VICTORIA UNIVERSITY PRESS
Victoria University of Wellington
PO Box 600 Wellington
vup.victoria.ac.nz

A catalogue record is available at the National Library of New Zealand

ISBN 9781776561957

Printed by Ligare, Auckland

To Meredith

Contents

2

3

1

There's No Place Like the Internet in Springtime

There's no place like the internet in springtime!
Everything foals a new thing like itself,
and old things are respectful in their pastures
and only argue over if it's best
to let the snow melt or to make it melt.
Vapours turn to rainbows and are praised
while flowers breathe out oxygen for days.
Wait, am I thinking of the internet?
Oh, maybe not, but what I'm thinking of
is desperate and very, very like it.
I have in mind new forms of intimacy
that sadly elude me and huddle with
the young. Across the distances they hum
like snow leopards and pandas falling in love.

Carlos Drummond's Truth Door

After Carlos Drummond de Andrade

The door of truth was open,
but, on account of the small room on the other side,
and there being nothing for propping
it open with, it only let through half a person at a time.

It was impossible to reach the whole truth at once,
as every person who tried was left, first, with a half-true face,
and then with another side that was differently half-true, so his
    or her countenance
was symmetrical but composite, like a breakfront bookcase.

So we smashed down the door.
We stepped into a bright place with brighter fires
and stacked dry cords of truth on the floor.
The place was also in two halves, despite the assertions of two-
    halves deniers

to the contrary. We came to discuss which was the lovelier side,
but both were fine, equally to be promoted and pitied,
so each of us chose as our isolated plight,
illusions, sense of timing, and short-sightedness permitted.

Four Directions at the Beach

Don't look back the way you came.
The whole new-built-up seaside is
a town of children and the barefoot
intellectually. The town seal
is sad Penelope weaving kelp.

The seaward view is very nice,
if you like hypnotherapy.
The waves can hold men listening
for hours even when the rain falls.
The wind benumbs and chaps and chills.

Look down into the turbid water.
The rushy swell that greens your feet
cuts you in half: half man, half corpse.
I found a wallet in the sea
today, lost since 2003.

But up! When you're floating on your back
and you look up, for once it's you
who's drifting in relation to
the sky. For once you listen
to yourself when no one else does.

I Am an Animal Benefiting from Climate Change

Finally these flippers, so clumsy out on the city's
fissured, hummocky asphalt, will steer me gracefully.
This skeleton I've worn inside these many years,
which should have been supported from deep below by the black,
dense, creatureless water of the abyssal zone,
but which instead has weighted and hindered and limited me,
with my only compensation thin air and some sunshine—
this structure that was grown can now be useful.
My helmeted crest of bone will frustrate all the desperate,
fleeing predators who'd club me on the bonce
and eat me at the kerb. Not that the path from killing
to eventually eating me is clear, or possible.
My skin, which rejects all touch and which has always pained me
more than any other (though it hurt others, too),
is adamant, and neither now nor in the future
will it give or let pass.
                      Because my body did not change
or even adjust to change, the change adjusted to me.
I lost one niche (confusion) and found another waiting.
The only happy surprise is a sudden survival advantage.
I can hardly give up that! And I don't mean to. Bye.
The hot, wet climate suits my hot, wet brain.
I'll remember all of you, and what you meant to me,
when the fossils of inland seas return to the water again.

A Line of Questioning

After Xenophanes

These questions should be saved for later,
when the mood is set,
in a library too lovely to read in,
when the fire is almost out,
but not yet,
and Rifkin's versions of Bach's cantatas are playing
like an angel's nasal hum,
and, for the greater good, we're drinking
a bottle from
the last cask from a lost distillery
on Islay, where the whisky was true and pure-hearted—
that's the time for saying:
'That's an interesting name. What does it mean?'
'How old are you now? How old were you then?'
'Where were you when the war started?'
'What's the worst thing you've ever seen?'

Double Saw Final at the Canterbury A&P Show

Grimacing, sunburnt blokes sawing the shit out of wood
for prizes—now that's sport. The mania of two people
contra-pulling one thing, trying to make a breakthrough,
a very literal break through the bottom of a pine log,
is like a conversation between matter and energy.
This front-and-back, powerful, achingly unctuous motion could be
the first step in making paper or a clock face,
but no—it's fine destruction. And as I watch I think
that, first, being the men, or, second, being the saw
would be the dream, either the agents or the tool
of the show's obliteration, but for poise and certainty,
pinioned in the sawbuck like a cylindrical, primitive statue
of a cast-off god, you can't beat the log.

A Classical Education

There were three classes of butchers
among the ancient Romans:
Suarii, *Boarii*, and *Lanii*—
for hogs, for cows, and for killing.
Some butchers wouldn't kill,
which even then was funny.

It was late before the Greeks
had any notion of butter,
and by the early Romans
it was only used as medicine—
never as food. Never as food.
There were oleaginous omens.

And I'm a fatted calf
in a town called Vitinia,
my first time in Europe.
I am still nineteen.
The picture is an altar scene
with one disgusting cherub.

The same night I picked up
an umbrella in a graveyard
and found a homeless person,
I ate a bad oyster.
Even after fifteen years
I don't know what I learned.

Uninstall Your News Apps and Join a Hiking Club

The way of man is froward and strange,
but are there any other options?
The only real suggestion box
is a room for being hypnotised in.
Some days I avoid a screen
for twenty minutes at a time,
but I don't count this time successful.
I can't even name the trees,
and I have to be in a special mood
to water the flowers with a squirt-gun
standing fifteen feet away.
I lurch back to what I know.
I do what I do because I do it.
I cloud my thoughts with news of the world.
It's like spooning a curry into a pool.
The misleading wisps and meaningful swirls
beguile me from the important questions:
How bright would something have to be
to make the sun cast a shadow?
How long would I actually have to live
to have the wind and sea erode me?

I Can't Even

A philosopher of Croton
wrote that how we differ
from the other creatures—
swollen in their ease,
half asleep at their salads—
is that we turn our agony
to account in sober creation.
So that cry you hear
is a sympathetic vibration
that out of the clashing forces
of life rings clear.
But wait, there's more.
The cry is a harmonic likeness
that becomes a metaphor.

The order within disorder
is a spice-rack in a shipwreck,
an abacus in the corner
at the ruined abbey of Glenluce,
or hill-roads amid the scree
where earthquakes preside.
It also is a probe
in orbit around a comet,
a self-tightening noose,
a precise polypeptide
in a gummy primordial soup;
it is phoning the cats on holiday
when the rain rains all day
and the pier is closed for the night.

The order within disorder
is like these things but isn't.
The things we write we transform:
the far becomes the distant,
the distant becomes the invisible,
the invisible becomes the new:
the new idea in town
that rings the bells at midnight
and pulls the statues down.
It's picked up by some and spread
and whispered at shadowy meetings
of threes or even twos
as though it were a godhead.
It's unbelievable if true.

All Cats Are Grey in the Dark

And all cold soups taste the same.
All mountains are gothic in the fog.
Every park looks pleasant from space.
When the inspectors aren't around, everything is a hot dog.

Every friendly jihadi is a 'moderate rebel'.
Ten starlings together look like a hawk.
Every antique shop is a care home for things.
Every state we help becomes Iraq.

Perception is not what we're good at,
though we think it is and say so.
A rich, inexchangeable set of experiences
has a street value of about one Cuban peso.

I'm Impressed

Long live the lazily conceived solution.
Wear snowshoes wrapped in cling-film underwater
or swim fins on the tundra or the piste.
See if I care. What's sort of good enough
is more than good enough for me, okay?
The human ingenuity I admire
is limited, implausible, post hoc,
folksy, unconsidered, overthought,
ecstatic, garden-shed, Corinthian,
exhausting, nebulous, and somehow sexy.
The person I would choose to lead my tribe
would build a whale by sewing some dolphins together,
and, by God, the honour of my life
would be to write the only click-to-whale-song /
whale-song-to-click dictionary
anyone will ever need.

Mailing in a Form Because There's No Online Form

In modern, safe societies, bureaucracy fills the role
that used to be filled by war. Instead of glaring across their borders,
  the whole
mass of massed peoples cringes at what surrounds it, like the nose
  of a star-nosed mole.

If soldiers no longer parade on the squares with leathery thwacks,
wearing cassowary plumes and Zouave trousers with legs like
  coffee sacks,
playing at war ('the gory nurse that trains societies to cohesiveness,'
  wrote William James a while back

before war meant what twentieth-century war meant),
it doesn't mean we have no common enemy. From seafloor vents
to revolving restaurants on top of skyscrapers, a force directs the
  management

of our lives. But while manipulation has been supervening
violence all these years, the rending of garments and lamentable
  keening
of powerless grief have only changed in magnitude and frequency
  and not in meaning.

In other words, it's not 'now, do what we say
and no one gets hurt,' it's 'do what we say and *you* won't get hurt,
  and anyway
you're far too busy today to worry about your fellow creatures'
  exponential decay.'

23

It's Nice

Who could be glum on a ferry?
It's nice to go basically nowhere
with everyone going there, too,
in their muffs and their snoods
and their good slippers (shoes).
It's the motion of it,
the pretending to do
what you could if you would
if you left Zuiderzoon.
And it's nice that you're not on the sea,
which you like, but it's long
and it smells of the East
and it tastes of the deep and its moods.
And nicest of all
the river is there
to be crossed and re-crossed
and it's never the same,
but it is (look it up).
By the time you worry
the world is too big
you're at Joost.
You've been confused,
but you've never been lost.

I Rank All the Beautiful Things There Are

I rank all the beautiful things there are
starting with self-sacrifice, then supernovas,
the brain, love, virga, Korean pottery,
lemurs, cuckoo clocks, suits of armour for horses,
a child's first words, mercy, bread, and so on.
The list extends for miles in knee-high piles
of pages I arrange on my weekends.
But then I think that comprehensiveness
is better served by a more encyclopaedic
presentation, so in the best morocco
I bind the beautiful things alphabetically.
The volumes cover fine segments of language,
limited like thin, bright bands of colour:
penumbra to pineapple, fox to funerals,
Rome to rum, *Antigone* to apricot.
Every shelf groans under the staggering weight
of another shelf, it seems. The accumulation
of items in fixed forms is knowledge itself.
But then I think that serendipity
is better served by digitising all
my lists and groupings. I put them in a folder—
the first step in putting them out of mind.
Five years pass and I remember them.
I look and realise all my views have changed.
I start again: with empathy, then music,
coral reefs, tornadoes, ice, titanium,
spoken Esperanto, things like that.
I interrogate my past like someone who's
set an exam for the examined life.

2

You Can't Teach Creative Writing

And yet I'm full of practical wisdom.
Like, I say there's 'good incongruity' in titles
and 'bad incongruity' in titles.
Good incongruity is 'Refrigerator on a Mountaintop'.
Bad incongruity is 'Injustice in the Toilet'.
But maybe I was born knowing this,
and maybe I was born knowing
that 'artisanship' is a lovely choriamb (/ x x /),
and maybe I was born knowing
that it's better to invent parents to write about
if yours are both real estate agents
who go on cruises for fun—
that's if you decide to write
an ambivalent family mood-piece
or a surly elegy at all,
which I would counsel against if I was teaching you.
And, really, how are you going to see anything
of Dubrovnik or Yangon in just a few hours
with that white cruise ship floating admonishingly in the harbour
like the bleaching skeleton of a chopped-down skyscraper?
No, if you want to really see Dubrovnik
you're going to have to live there,
in the alleys and wynds and mews,
and that, metaphorically speaking, is my advice to you,
writer who wonders if writing can be taught:
move to Dubrovnik.

The Family Lore Poem

On Christmas Day, 1930, my father's uncle,
Willie Dowall, then a striker for Motherwell FC,
got the call that made him not-a-striker for Motherwell FC,
but not a former player of Motherwell FC
either. And so he moved along the path
that saw him finally able to hold down a place
as Motherwell's right back in 1931–32,
a versatile man in a memorable year, when half of Lanarkshire
whooped it up for the Well winning the league,
and half of Lanarkshire was raddled and out of work,
and the third half were Hamilton Academical fans.
The player who replaced him at the front, another Willie—
because every Scottish William was a Willie
the moment he laced up boots to run on grass,
even (or especially) when he was called Bill in England—
the gunstock-jawed Willie MacFadyen, still holds
the Scottish league single-season scoring record (52).
Please let all the less accomplished strikers form an
       orderly queue.
You know what they say: like holding a cat's paw,
accepting the greatness of others *should* be easy, but it's hard.
The thirties became the forties, rivalries became hostilities,
and Willie died before the championship team reunion,
many years later, a time for the boys to think through
how they used their bodies to strike or save
when all the men still smoked, and some of the steelworks did, too.

Your Grandfather's War Stories

It's just as well they're lost. If there are no details,
　　there is no elegist
or interpreter required. The three possibilities are:
　　1) He was a hero.
He saved a Belgian nun or stopped some Hittite chariots
　　with his Lewis gun.
Luckiness like this is very unlikely to be
　　found in a family twice.
It's a distinction you can't borrow. Makes you think, huh?
　　2) He was a horror.
He slew a paddock of cows and smashed the wings of idols
　　and torched a monastic house
while either following orders or otherwise ordering followers.
　　He marched over the borders
of Anecdote to Shame, not for his life or an edge.
　　3) He was a cipher.
He pulled a trireme oar and bayonetted straw
　　and practised semaphore
under a grand palm tree and sorted Hannibal's letters
　　and got the French disease
and spotted German planes and wrote for the regiment magazine.
　　Like a hurricane,
the paperwork zone destroys with low pressure.
　　The unknown story contains
all possible themes, just as a war contains
　　the potential for peace.

The Shame

The shame adhered like flour on dark trousers:
un-flick-off-able. The shame lay down
along a heated rock and sunned itself
because it could, because the right to bask
is respected in all civilised countries.
The shame ate and ate until it got hungry
again and helped itself—no need to ask!
The shame, at its work desk, busied itself
from the minute when the lights came on in town
to the hour when the lights went out in houses.

Public Power

The public streets, the private houses—all
are lit as if they lived inside the internet.
But there are horses in the public streets,
and in the private houses lurks the whooping cough,
and at the Star in Church Street is a man
who says he fought against Napoleon. Perhaps he did.
For this is Godalming in 1881.

Two waterwheels are powered by the Wey
and drive a generator. This is how the town
can buy and use its electricity,
which no city or town has ever done before.
The streets are bright. The lanes are dimly bright.
The parlours are as bright as Father can afford to make them.
For this is Godalming in 1881.

The quality of light, the quality
of life . . . a popular elision, but a good one.
The light is valued for its truthiness.
The light is mother of the truth. The empire grows
like a maturing star, or so it thinks.
A good thing happens here because it's meant to happen here.
For this is Godalming in 1881.

The Great Sunspot of 1947

Around the breakfast table
the family hear the news:
'Record Sunspot Seen'.
It's on all the radios
and in the *Intelligencer*.
Exactly what it means
is carefully explained.
It affects the rates of loans,
the mysterious sunspot cycle.
The best Rhenish wines
are made in sunspot years.
Trees grow, and vines,
and rabbit populations
explode, stabilise, explode.
Viruses may mutate,
radios go cold
as storms hit the earth.
More children will be born,
not immaculately, today,
but as a matter of course:
it's the greatest ever sunspot.
And yet there are things
it's unconnected to.
The cycle doesn't bring
madness upon the land,
a strife upon the house,
or sorrow to a table,
or pettiness, abuse,
cowardice or error.

According to the reports,
morals are unaffected.
Scientists of the heart
and brain rest easy.
The people who report
may be breathless, mad and keen,
but take heart, take heart!
Peter, Barb and Susan,
around the breakfast table,
know that your little lives
are unassailable wholes.
The woes are in the details,
the details are in the woes.

An Abandoned Farm Near Lockhart, New South Wales

The shearing shed is in good order,
and if it strongly smells of piss
and hums with every kind of fly
there is, at least the tools still work.
The heat outside makes me want to die;
in here I'm sure I have already.
Twenty-year-old wool appears
from among the roofbeams when I cough.
There is no black that's blacker than
a wool that's changed to black.
I say that we should turn the place
into a working farm museum,
but I try to turn everything
into a museum. Yet still
the moment and the sentiment
are right. They feel so right to me.
Of course they do. I have the hands
and posture of a visitor.
What I'm saying is all ego,
and that's not what farming is or was.
(According to what I am told.)
It's selling rather than keeping things,
killing to sell, nurturing to kill,
and letting self-control be nurtured.
(That's what I'm told by those who know.)
The rising damp eats the dado.

And in the garden by the house,
persevering, unreliant on
the absent gardener: plumbago.

Georgics

A lambent light it is that fills the pasture, but it's too dark to read.
The wise farmer rises early to get the best broadband speed.

As shepherds watch their fleecy care, they see claggy-arsed,
    beady-eyed billows of wool.
A full house is a pair of Cheviots and three of a kind of Karakuls.

'Pneumatic nipple suck-fest' is a quaint term for the morning
    milking!
Gervase Markham writes of a cow that filled sixty buckets.

You can ride a tractor from, as the Italians say, the stable to
    the stars.
The tractor's GPS is more powerful than the computer on the
    ship that, some day, will take men to Mars.

Fifty miles south of here it's green-yellow. Fifty miles north
    it's green.
Here, brown trout are scooped from the drying river in nets and
    trucked to the sea.

They wrap hay in plastic now, another processed food.
'They' are the farmers. Making hay is a pleasant interlude.

The last lightning-strike fire was put out by passing farmer
    Alan MacHugh.
The superstitious among us say that he threw the lightning
    himself.

I've asked, and my duty is not to protect the weak.
It is to make the weak strong. May they use that strength to
make their own peace.

At night, from a car, sheep's eyes look like the ghosts of
snooker balls.
The dew falls in orbs and rises in a vaporous pyramid. That's
the water cycle, kid.

The half-sun on the evening hill is a great aunt's hairy kiss.
Around the manger the animals sing 'What Version of Pastoral
Is This?'

Where the glow-worm creepeth in the night, no adder will go in
the day.
The ways things are going now, it's cheaper to throw the crops
out than to give them away.

Poem in Which, in Which, in Which

In which a couple of lines will be read which came, perhaps, from the Evil One.

In which the reader learns that this story is told not from forethought, but through a common chance of life.

In which are contained divers reasons why a man should not write in a hurry.

In which the author makes small progress in his journey; but wherein he endeavours to make amends in other ways.

In which the polite reader may very possibly find an image of himself; and concluding with a piece of advice especially intended to go round the upper circles.

In which a fairy in a cotton-print dress is introduced.

In which the affection of a humble friend manifests itself.

In which comes a wind which blows nobody good.

In which 'misfortunes never come singly'.

In which some light is thrown upon some circumstances which were before rather mysterious.

In which we change the scene, and the sex of our performers.

In which a point of some delicacy is started.

In which much is developed.

In which a radical change of atmosphere is at once noticed.

In which there is much joy and some work.

In which the reader assists at some religious services, intermixed with dancing and sundry recreations.

In which we enjoy three courses and a dessert.

In which the party receives a new impetus.

In which a sudden stop is put to the music.

In which a heavenly witness appears who cannot be cross-examined, and before which the defense utterly breaks down.

In which the reader will perceive that in some cases madness
   is catching.
In which the last act of a comedy takes the place of the first.
In which the readerkin will, if he has an ounce of brains, begin
   to catch the inevitable denoumong of the imbroglio.
In which the author himself makes his appearance on the stage.
In which post-mortem processions are spoken of.
In which is shewn how the torch of hope blazes to the last, and
   makes around it an atmosphere of light and life.
In which the author became convinced that he was no longer
   upon the earth.
In which the Sphinx sleeps forever.

The Paris Agreement

Again in a time of negligible public trust
the important thing is to trust. If we don't believe
the treaty-makers, they won't believe themselves.
The phrase that nearly broke the deal was just
what you'd expect: every translator knows
a delicate word for 'we are so fucked'
but none for 'legally enforceable'.
In the bleak mild winter, discussions close.
For one person, a hoop is just a hoop
to jump through, but for 196 parties
it's a multi-meaning, omni-deployable
torus of the imagination. Oops.
It will never not be right to panic.
Meanwhile, we array our satisfied brains
flaccid and cool and semi-supine like a hammock
slung between two candy canes.

Growing Fears That the Leadership Contest Has Been Hijacked by Far-Left Infiltrators

If you think that spiny lobsters
should own
the spiny lobster migration paths
and not some groaning sea-god
who licenses his image
for use in tuna ads and myths,

and if you believe a turtle shell
with dozens
of turtles trying to get in, crying
'We're all in it together!'
is what the world will look like
in about 2029,

and if the chambered nautilus
to you
represents a way of coping
with a repeated loss of home
instead of a ropey scheme
for having loads of extra bedrooms,

and if in your entire life
you've had
no one to identify with
who wasn't first and last
a danger to the good
through well-meaning compromise,

if you can agree to this,
resignedly but definitely,
you might be a socialist.

Dickheads in an Election Year

The casting vote always rests
with the voter who votes with a gun.
You can have a cloud of octopuses;
it's a squid that squirts the ink.

The ink is supposed to be e-ink now,
but I won't give up vellum.
An illuminated manuscript
is the best bedtime read.

In *The Perfect Crime*, Jean Baudrillard
solves the 'murder of reality'.
The murder weapon is virtuality;
his client, the academy.

Some of my best friends are bankers,
says the man who lives in a vault.
The penny should be made of Valium,
not copper and cum and zinc.

What do you think? Instead of letting the few
ruin it for everyone,
why not just let everyone
ruin it for the few?

That's what I'll do, if elected,
and if elected I'll serve.
You get the leadership you deserve,
and then it deserves you.

Some Anglophone Poetry

Americans enthuse over theory they use to make themeless
    theremin music,

while

bristly British critics criticise brutish stichic exercises.

The Democracy Sonnet

This is not democracy. This is a seal balancing a tesseract on its
  nose and barking for chocolate fish.
This is not democracy. This is a nightclub with the word
  Bibliothèque carved in the stone above the entrance.
This is not democracy. This is a shoal named after the captain who
  first grounded on it by his gleeful rival.
This is not democracy. This is an armillary sphere showing
  a cosmos of many gods orbiting one worshipper in elaborate
  epicycles.
This is not democracy. This is the guestbook on Ladies' Night at
  the show trials.
This is not democracy. This is a ticket machine playing slow jazz
  with your slip as your train departs for True Love.
This is not democracy. This is a ghillie suit hanging on a hat-stand
  in the living room at an austerity-pickled Christmas.
This is not democracy. This is the honeybee faking its own death
  worldwide.
This is not democracy. This is an ancient artefact grudgingly
  repatriated from a museum to its country of origin.
This is not democracy. This is your lovingly built childhood
  dollhouse left out in the rain by mobsters to 'send you a message'.
This is not democracy. This is your ancestor known in his youth
  for torturing priests and in his age for founding churches.
This is not democracy. This is a cactus and an echeveria in a
  terrarium fighting over a beautiful pebble.
This is not democracy. This is a twist in a mystery story with a card
  game no one plays.
This is not democracy. This is a flood lasting no nights and
  somehow lasting forty days.

A Spam Christmas

Asian singles, Jewish singles, Black singles, Nordic singles, singles
from above the Arctic Circle will put a lucky sixpence in your
Christmas pudding.

Take tinsel supplements to feel thirty again. To feel three again. To
feel the age you were when you last got a present you loved.

Start with a solid roof over your head with tinsel shingles. Fill the
garden with tinsel fertiliser. Fuck like a tinsel snowman this season.

Reverse-mortgage the house with the tinsel-filled garden.

Take a trip to Africa this Christmas and shoot a stripy reindeer.
These storage devices will hold your special memories.

A tactical flashlight is the perfect gift for someone dim, for someone
who might want to be run over by a dump truck and survive, or
be frozen in a block of ice and still illuminate a burglar.

Not everyone who breaks into your house this December will be Santa
Claus. That's why there are carbon-fibre crossbows. Hang on, not
crossbows—CrossFit-affiliated gyms.

Dear patriots, shed those holiday pounds fast by enlisting in the army
today. No one remembers how that Christmas cracker joke went,
but the answer is: 'An army marches on its stomach.'

Improve your golf swing, golf swingers, golf swingles, golf swingle-
bells, please keep improving, especially at this time of year when

those in need feel want most keenly.

Learn new languages fast. 'Tinsel' in Japanese is *tinseru*. 'Tinsel' in Portuguese is *ouropel*. 'Tinsel' in German is *lametta*. 'Tinsel' in Georgian is *polga*.

Put the X-ACTO knife back in Xmas.

Put the X-Men back in Xmas.

Put the Jaguar XJ back in Xmas.

Put the X-ray technicians' jobs back in Xmas.

There is a war on, a goddamned war on Christmas, so get your food delivered by drone.

You don't have to be told how valuable your time is, and that includes your time on earth. Get more coverage for less money by only singing religious carols, which are frankincense to secular carols' frankfurters.

Fool the police with this one easy trick: eat eighty liquor-filled chocolates while crying on the carpet.

In the bleak midwinter, inspiration goes.

What's red and white and green with envy? A candy cane when it hears how I made $2,611 working from home today.

Tentative Readings

And let us pity now the unimpeachable makers of art,
who suffer on account of the substitution fallacy,
which holds that every work is secretly another work,
as sulphur is stealthily gold, and Tony Abbott a lizard man.
So 'Stopping by Woods on a Snowy Evening' now is *about* death,
and *Jaws* is *about* Watergate or very Watergate-like,
and 'Shit Arm, Bad Tattoo' by Half Man Half Biscuit
is *about* Pete Doherty—this could possibly be right
to one who treats a literary theory like a scarf,
placed in a drawer or on a chilly throat but never both.
This is what happens when you over-privilege the heart,
which generates the intensely boring monomaniac passions—
you over-privilege the heart because you only have a heart.

Remembering America

The question 'Do you miss it?' is unanswerable.
It's obscene to say *yes*. It's depressing to others to say *no*.
It's inauthentic and invertebrate to say *maybe*.
I'd rather sing 'Oh baby, oh baby, oh baby' in a song
than answer it. I have attempted just to name things
I have liked in my location-limited experience,
like fried clams as big as men's watch-faces
or a turkey jumping majestically over my father's bicycle wheel
or suburban snowmen bathing in the cold light of flat-screen TVs,
but that doesn't answer the question 'Do you miss it?'
any more than 'I believe I was a cat in a past life'
answers the question 'How do you feel?'
Prove to me that the country I thought I grew up in
was real. You can't unless you beguile me
with your fireworky thinking, your monster-truck cunning,
your whispers of calumny that you cast like the peal of
   a cracked bell
across the prairies I've never been to
and the peninsulas I have been to
and the places I've been to and forgotten everywhere.
Missing something is a state of mind,
says the polar bear on her shrinking ice floe.
Knowing not to miss it is a state of grace,
says the hermit crab in her rented carapace.
America, like a lot of people, I'm keeping my distance,
as we do from a super-volcano on public land.
America, a house haunted by itself cannot stand.
America, you are a monument to monumental misrepresentation,
and all your monuments should commemorate this.

America, you're apostrophised so much
because you're still not listening.
America, you look even worse from somewhere else
than you do from inside yourself.

3

Some Fixations (in the Northern Spring)

We act out randomly
to bring our objects near.
It's eighteen degrees and birds
are frequenters of the air
again. They don't know why,
but they thought of little else
while they were in the tropics,
wearing yellow belts
of frank and faithful feathers.
The symptoms don't show
to the one who actually has them,
and a bagpiper I know
is always munching carrots,
proving that his mouth
does what the head knows not.
And now they fly back south,
the birds I mentioned above,
and despite my unconcern
about where they have gone
some day they'll reaffirm
my unfelt fascination.
I'm thinking about, soon,
or maybe even next time,
communicating with you.

Letter from the Estuary

Two feet of snow at my parents' place, in another season.
Here, the cicadas sing like Christian women's choirs
in a disused cotton mill. Belief is a kind of weather.
I haven't seen proper snow for three years.

The new urban forest for native plants and birds
will be splendid if the local cats don't kill the birds.
The problem is, all my sympathies are with the cats.
The friendly disturbers are more endearing than what
    they disturb.

A trimaran called *3rd Degree* spinning around its cable in
    the channel:
that's how love is here and should be everywhere.
It seems so unserious or contentedly ironic;
it's the kind of thing you either look through or ignore.

But you'd be wrong. The question isn't: Why is love so
    strange here?
It's: Why did it feel normal somewhere else?
In quiet places, the present is just gossip about the past.
The future is a critique of that. All my best.

Love Poem with Seagull

I wish I'd seen it from your side of the table

when the horrid gull attacked my fish and chips,

the springy baton of haddock in my hand

a signal for the post-saurian psycho

to swoop at my talonless fingers as they moved towards my mouth

in their classically dithering mammalian way,

because if I'd had the privilege to see

the stress-warped, flexuous face behind

my bat-like ultrasonic shrieks of shock

as I fought off the bird unsuccessfully

then I'd have some idea of what it means

for you to love me, the sort of person who manages

to always look like this or feel like this

regardless of how much easier being normal is.

Amores

It's hard to love someone for who they are, so we dress up
    for weddings.
The wave withdraws from around your feet, and your toes
    cause the biggest eddies.

The scientific consensus is: No screens in bed.
This new bamboo pillow lets me forget that I have a head.

Moving in with someone marks a 'strange new stage of life'.
I used to wait until the fruits were ripe to pick them off
    the greengage.

Those tree branches shaped like lovers' swings cup the buttocks
    just right.
They describe a parabola that goes, returningly, from night to
    erotic night.

When they melt down the love locks from the Pont des Arts,
    they can build a tank.
But do I look like the sort of guy who'd accept a ride from a
    stranger in a tank?! No thanks.

Trying to control who the control freak is in a two-control-
    freak relationship
is a form of democratic dictatorship (according to an unofficial
    leak).

Oh, why does the sun, that meddling twonk, rise before our
    alarm, my darling?

I remember when dawn was a thing a private security firm was
    supposed to be guarding.

An illicit brothel has opened in England Street, and it's 'as busy
    as McDonald's'.
It's an amusingly small bottleneck through which the desires
    are funnelled.

Take the years you've spent alone and multiply them by five.
    That's your real age.
Turquoise's complementary colour is beige, so forget it! Do the
    nursery in Spanish white.

Soviet lander *Luna 18* lies in a heap forever at the edge of the
    Sea of Fertility.
Now that's what I call emotion recollected in tranquillity.

I think it was Lucretius who said that falling in love is like
    having drunk three bottles of wine the night before,
and that love is actually all we can eat or drink, and that's what
    makes us omnivores.

Wasting Time

If you think about a lost day,

I hope you have no regrets.

It's easy once you know the steps.

1) Lose something.

2) Don't know what it is you've lost.

3) Be above it all, like a snowstorm

stage-whispering about the frost.

Varnishing at Night

Here's a thing I understand:
the outrage some of you would feel
to see our neighbours varnishing
their smart new cladding under the lights
they've set up solely for the purpose.

I don't know why they're doing it, either.
I do know that the urgency,
the panting urgency to finish,
without a deadline or a reason,
is what we call a 'modern sickness'.

I also know that the private anger
of distant readers and close neighbours
narrows in gut-clenchingly
on those whose motives are unseen
and whose defences are incomplete.

How a New Zealand Sunrise Is Different
from Other Sunrises

Pinks and yellows collude to orange the hillside,
but they trick you into thinking the hills are proper orange
on their own, like an oystercatcher's lurid bill,
which grew that way, and not like a Riccarton tanner's arse,
which is art, not nature unimproved and wild.

Pinks and yellows collude to orange the air
like Jurassic sap from kauri that became Otago amber,
and in that amber are the fossils of tiny, boring beasts,
but instead of in amber the light is trapped in coastal moisture,
and instead of fossils two haggard gulls hang in the glow.

Pinks and yellows collude to orange the sea
in a navigational way, as orange as the buoys
that mark the channel to the yacht club in the estuary,
from which anyone might voyage early in the earth's day
when the 'first' sunrise reaffirms the tyranny of time zones.

Pinks and yellows collude to orange your face,
upturned and east-turned just before commuting time,
and you look like a boiled roadcone, a punchbowl with
    a hundred drinks
of Drambuie and pineapple in it, a haunted persimmon,
a never-to-be-longlisted alternative flag of bruised saffron tints.

The School of Naps

A nap on the farm was as common as a two-headed sheep.
This is why Meredith never learned to nap.
I, on the other hand, was encouraged to dream whenever
I wanted. In naps or in nap-like afternoons I smothered
in imagination. An only child is the parent of its parents,
a dictator with a small bedroom. I guess they had coherence,
those days in the close suburban yards and modest shrubberies
when I imposed my will on my impractical, summery
family. I've always had trouble getting things done since.
I seem to be walking along a floor mounted on springs.
When you're happy you have a responsibility to those who
      are unhappy
to do your best with it. Even if it ends badly.
Most of my choices are bad and good interspersed,
like wearing a motorcycle helmet while riding a horse.

Get a Pet with a Longer Lifespan Than Humans Have

Get a pet with a longer lifespan than humans have.
Treat yourself to a minimal expectation of sorrow
for once. Think of your children inheriting $36
plus a venerable pet, and how this will assuage their grief.

Let it gaze at you in that easy way the immortals have.
'For you, eerie friend, I'll never cry and never pity,'
you'll say. And with the psychic energy you'll save,
you can know yourself ten percent better or learn to keep bees.

What Customer Feedback Forms Filled Out by Your Friends Say About You

Gerta loves me but not anything about me, and that's
    pretty common.
Laura says I'm nice and actually doesn't write anything else,
    so she's dead to me.
Antoine's feelings about me look like love to the fanciful eye as
    the amygdala, to the anatomists who named it, resembled an
    almond.
Fidencio hopes I get better soon, as if I've just had an
    appendectomy.

Bunny resents being put in this position and implies that I'd
    prefer an abridgement of the truth.
Heidi is amazed that, if I want to do it, I'm allowed.
Masha sticks to my relative tallness and relative youth.
Zenobia awards me all the stars and draws me sitting atop, or
    perhaps emitting, a cloud.

Ramesh declares that giving my anorak a name means I have
    intimacy issues.
Corinna notices that I make every inconvenience a test.
Elle respects my respect for traditions, but she's not sure how
    much is tradition and how much is my own addition.
Ning says only an only child would mewl for praise as much as
    I do, and she's right—don't I do that the best?

Oona thinks we met in 2009, but it was 2004.
Val imagines my death, probably smothered by ten thousand

moths while changing a light bulb because I won't listen to
    advice.
Queenie wonders about my posture: do I sleep on my back on a
    Methodist church floor?
Ursula describes my smile: the tentative expression of someone
    who's just won a year's supply of pork fried rice.

Isabelle writes: 'Seventy years ago, everyone made tea as good
    as yours, but you're the only real tea-maker left.'
Trevor, the shit, unimpressed with my honesty, compares me
    to a ship that's built in South Korea but takes Liberian
    nationality.
Xenia comments on my race: to quote an obscure Victorian,
    I'm as white as the virgin snow of an Alpine cleft.
Yoni admires my thunderstorm-on-a-summer-afternoon-in-the-
    tropics-like punctuality.

Will wishes that just for once I could see what other people see:
    a brilliant, warm, charming, generous, creative loser.
Prasanna is so kind about that thing I do with my neck.
Jessica thinks I should worry less about people I've just met and
    focus on the end-user.
Dougal suggests that I take all my old heartaches and bury
    them in a cromlech.

Sonia thinks I'm vain but sees herself in that.
Kiyoko would like me better if I was a cat.

The Contentment Poem

So the lawnmower ran out of fuel halfway through the mow
revealing in the two-toned, two-height fescue grass
my tendency to cut a backwards L or a flat J
absentmindedly as I pootle along the lawn,
which now is the despair of neighbourhood dogs who live
    at lawn-height,
and also of their owners, whom I'm suspicious of
because *they're* never at lawn-height or dog-height or
    human-height,
instead surveying the street from the level of summer clouds;
anyway, these owners, seeing what I've done
to maintain our private sward in the expected way,
and seeing what looks like a sudden, small dogleg golf hole
with equal parts rough and vaguely inviting fairway,
and knowing a little of what I'm like from passing me by
semi-voluntarily every week of their lives,
these owners may think, just may think,
I've got the garden just how I like it and that, obviously,
is just how I like it.

Tropics Pub

Fans are fans and hot is hot;
one to another feeling
what's wet and what's not
under the big sky wheeling
over the sozzling hot!
Nights are drunk here:
we fill up, we cheer, courage spots
caution and there's a stained thought
of that night, again. We're near
our limits. But to be *we* means
never to be still
the way we were, to dream
as far as farther Bougainville,
to love what we forgot.

Imagining Ageing. Reimagining Ageing

The images are all of tortoises
and cactuses, iguanas and dry leaf.
Indifferently, the body moves along,
indulged though being slow and dull and safe,
indulged for being slow and dull and safe.
The wearing years have let the body keep
a funny but acceptable number of teeth.

It's different when the body isn't safe.
Serene and indefatigable herds
of grazers graze and graze and outcompete
anything weaker than a bomb with feet.
The closing years have shut the body up.
Pain comes for the first time and fear returns.
The mouth has changed completely and so have the words.

The Self-Esteem Poem

How can we know the weather balloon from the weather?
Well, one gets reported and forecast
and studied and hated and talked about dutifully whether

or not it's interesting, whereas the other
is ignored unless it explodes.
Whichever one you think you are, you're the other.

My Repetitive Strain Injury

I hurt my mind thinking of you.
I hurt my mind thinking of you.
You were far away and I
was where I was in that grey time.

It's not getting better, it's getting worse.
It's not getting better, it's getting worse
because I give it no rest.
I make it turn and tango and twist.

No one knows how to treat this.
No one knows how to treat this,
but it doesn't stop them giving advice:
'Think other thoughts.' 'Be someplace else.'

You don't have to let it hold you back,
you don't have to let it hold you back,
they say. Until there is a cure,
accommodate, adapt, endure.

Last Words

It's only wise
to set down in advance
a final footnote to a life,
an unequivocal surmise,
an answer to credit
for the student of your story,
which ends not now but soon.
Soon?! Sooner than the meaning
that you make will die,
and sooner than your least idea,
which lives in all the little thinkers
of your class and time
who put it just that way
and mean it just as you did.
It may be autumn now,
but the trees are not denuded.

Some words like these, perhaps:
'I give this life
that others may live givingly.'
Or 'As I am flesh,
devour me, O toothful God!'
Or 'The next road may be long
to travel but it's free.'
Or 'Every rejection
is a chance to resubmit.'
Or 'There are no accidents:
the only death is the death of sense.'
Some words like these,

to help to soothe a kindly soul
who watches a career,
and family, and seekers of truth,
and the casually curious afteryears.

Else there's a risk
of leaving with a dwindling gasp,
a rattled 'Here endureth',
a hurtling, quacked-out panic
as this leaden pall
that descends and hoods the eyes
tightens round the throat.
I hate surprises.
The possibility, however remote,
to be remembered quote-unquote
the right way
is one flutter, one spring,
one chance-directed beat
among them all
from the wings of many birds
in many paradises.

Because it is
a hopeful animal
that writes its days down,
and a yearning one
that writes to future days,
I can smile as I sigh.
And the ultimate refinement

of the rarest funereal thought
is confected commonplace,
which only glitters
brighter than but doesn't
taste the stronger when compared
to what one writes in a reflective mood
in a diary or phone,
to the effect of:
I cared, I cared, I cared, I cared.

Today

The rabbit does not hop in her brisk way.
The artist can't imagine anything.
The hill declines the tenderness of fogs.
The soap diminishes in many hands.
The car refuses once again to start.
The isotope continues to decay.
The chair awaits the sitter, who is late.
The building segregates its occupants.
The cliff resigns an outcrop to the sea.
The window jams and won't let in the breeze.
The mould spores screw their way into the bread.
The tree ignores its greeny symmetry.
The dog laments her owner in the yard.
And I, alone and glad, have missed these things.

Notes

'Carlos Drummond's Truth Door' is a loose translation of Carlos Drummond de Andrade's poem 'Verdade', which can be found in *Poesia completa* (Nova Aguilar: Rio de Janeiro, 2002).

'A Line of Questioning' is based on the Xenophanes fragment beginning, in John Burnet's 1892 translation, 'Now is the floor clean . . .'

'Public Power' was written for *For Every Year*, Crispin Best's online project that brings together one purpose-written poem for every calendar year since 1400. In 1881, Godalming, Surrey, became the first town in the world to have a public electricity supply.

The abandoned farm near Lockhart, New South Wales, is called Woodlands, and it is where my partner, Meredith, grew up. Coincidentally, I grew up in a street called Woodland Road.

The title 'Growing Fears That the Leadership Contest Has Been Hijacked by Far-Left Infiltrators' comes from a (demented) *Telegraph* article from 27 July 2015.

The events of 'Love Poem with Seagull' took place in Hastings (the one in East Sussex, not the one in Hawke's Bay) on the day after Britain's EU referendum. This is why the fish mentioned is haddock, which does not live in southern seas. The poem was tentatively titled 'The Battle of Hastings' before I thought better of it.

Each of the 28 lines of 'Poem in Which, in Which, in Which' is drawn from a literary source, as follows:

1) *Les Misérables*, 1862, Victor Hugo, trans. Charles E. Wilbour.

2) *Lady Beauty, or Charming to Her Latest Day*, 1882, Alan Muir.

3) *A History of New-York, from the Beginning of the World to the End of the Dutch Dynasty*, 1821, Washington Irving.

4) *Rambles in the Footsteps of Don Quixote*, 1837, Henry David Inglis.

5) *Adventures of Bilberry Thurland*, 1836, Charles Hooton.

6) *Jessie Trim*, 1874, Benjamin Leopold Farjeon.

7) *Margaret Ravenscroft, or Second Love*, 1835, James Augustus St John.

8) *Vagabondia*, 1884, Frances Hodgson Burnett.

9) *Otterstone Hall*, 1884, Urquhart Atwell Forbes.

10) *Henrietta Temple*, 1837, Benjamin Disraeli.

11) *Snarleyyow, or the Dog Fiend*, 1837, Frederick Marryat.

12) *The Life and Adventures of George St Julian, the Prince of Swindlers*, 1844, Henry Cockton.

13) *Was He Successful?*, 1863, Richard B. Kimball.

14) *The Little Red Chimney, Being the Love Story of a Candy Man*, 1914, Mary Finley Leonard.

15) *Julia Ried*, 1872, Isabella Macdonald Alden.

16) *Asmodeus in New-York*, 1868, Ferdinand Longchamp.

17) *Vanity Fair*, 1848, William Makepeace Thackeray.

18) *His Lordship's Leopard*, 1900, David Dwight Wells.

19) *Haunted Hearts*, 1864, Maria Susanna Cummins.

20) *Sevenoaks, a Story of Today*, 1875, Josiah Gilbert Holland.

21) *Sir Launcelot Greaves*, 1760, Tobias Smollett.

22) *The Ordeal of Richard Feverel*, 1859, George Meredith.

23) *The Green Overcoat*, 1912, Hilaire Belloc.

24) *The History of Tom Jones, a Foundling*, 1749, Henry Fielding.

25) *Sense, or Saturday-Night Musings and Thoughtful Papers*, 1868, Brick Pomeroy.

26) *Tom Bowling*, 1841, Frederick Chamier.

27) *Armata: A Fragment*, 1817, Thomas Erskine.

28) *The House of the Sphinx*, 1907, Henry Ridgely Evans.

Acknowledgements

Poems in this book have appeared (sometimes in slightly different forms) in the following journals:

Antiphon: 'It's Nice'

Berfrois: 'A Spam Christmas'

Catalyst: 'I Can't Even', 'The Democracy Sonnet'

The Dark Horse: 'Love Poem with Seagull'

Dead King Magazine: 'Mailing in a Form Because There's No Online Form'

For Every Year: 'Public Power'

The Interpreter's House: 'Your Grandfather's War Stories'

The Island Review: 'Four Directions at the Beach'

Ladowich: 'There's No Place Like the Internet in Springtime', 'Uninstall Your News Apps and Join a Hiking Club', 'Get a Pet with a Longer Lifespan Than Humans Have'

Landfall: 'Georgics', 'Amores', 'How a New Zealand Sunrise Is Different from Other Sunrises', 'Today'

LEVELER: 'The School of Naps'

The Manchester Review: 'I Rank All the Beautiful Things There Are', 'An Abandoned Farm Near Lockhart, New South Wales'

Ohio Edit: 'The Paris Agreement'

Poems in Which: 'Poem in Which, in Which, in Which'

Poetry: 'Letter from the Estuary'

Prelude: 'The Shame'

PUBLIC POOL: 'Dickheads in an Election Year', 'What Customer Feedback Forms Filled Out by Your Friends Say About You'

Sport: 'Carlos Drummond's Truth Door', 'I Am an Animal Benefiting from Climate Change', 'A Line of Questioning', 'Double Saw Final at the

Canterbury A&P Show', 'Imagining Ageing. Reimagining Ageing'

And the following anthologies:

Leaving the Red Zone (Clerestory Press, 2016): 'Varnishing at Night'

Poets for Corbyn (a *Berfrois* e-book, 2015): 'Growing Fears That the Leadership Contest Has Been Hijacked by Far-Left Infiltrators'

I am grateful to all the editors and readers.

———

As this is my first book, I believe I am entitled to go on a thanking spree. It's a tradition.

Thanks to Meredith Henderson for everything—and I do mean everything.

Thanks to Julia, Jocelyn, Gerry, Pushkin, Tolstoy, Boswell and Larkin, the last four of whom are very fine cats.

Thanks to George and Susan Kennedy for the endless opportunities I was given to imagine.

Thanks to Doc Drumheller and Ciaran Fox. Thanks to John Allison, Wade Bishop, Teresa Correia, Andy Coyle, Merissa Foryani, Cassandra Fusco, Stephanie Hacksley, Roger Hickin, Jeffrey Paparoa Holman, Rose Journeaux, Melanie McKerchar, John Newton, James Norcliffe, John O'Brien, Joanna Preston, Claire Thompson and Tam Vosper.

Thanks to Marisa Cappetta, Jeni Curtis, Catherine Fitchett and Chris Stewart.

Thanks to Cornelia Barber, Russ Bennetts, Rauan Klassnik and Ruben Quesada.

Thanks to Shawn Adler, Patrick Carr, Peter Geller, Clayton Lamar and Ian MacAllen for their friendship back in those vital formative years.

Thanks to Ashleigh Young, Fergus Barrowman, Kirsten McDougall and the rest of the VUP juggernaut for believing that this work should be out in the world and taking steps to make that happen. Not many things can make being a poet any easier, but a great press is one of them.